Quiet at the Edge

poems by

Deborah Casillas

Finishing Line Press
Georgetown, Kentucky

Quiet at the Edge

ACKNOWLEDGMENTS

With gratitude to the editors of the following publications where these
poems first appeared:

The Carolina Quarterly: "Enigma of Stone and Line," Mesa of Wind and
Unceasing Light," and "The Undefined"

The Whitefish Review: "Wild Irises"

Under the Volcano/Bajo el Volcán anthology: "Red Warbler," and "Would You
Buy a Soul"

Much gratitude to Lise Goett for her support and advice in ordering the
manuscript, and for her critiques of the many poems that emerged from
her generative workshops. Gratitude as well to Mary Morris for her careful
reading and helpful comments on early versions of the manuscript.

Publisher: Leah Maines
Editor: Christen Kincaid
Cover Art: Kay Harvey
Author Photo: J. B. Smith
Cover Design: Elizabeth Maines McCleavy

Printed in the USA on acid-free paper.
Order online: www.finishinglinepress.com
　　　　　also available on amazon.com

Author inquiries and mail orders:
Finishing Line Press
P. O. Box 1626
Georgetown, Kentucky 40324
U. S. A.

Table of Contents

IV

for Adam and Christian

i.

Revelations

For how many years had my eye
failed me, and now, transformed

by technology, by genius—
that slight incision, the quick insertion—

a kaleidoscope dancing above the slit,
rainbow, fireworks, shooting stars—

I will behold again the glorious spectrum
dimmed so long. The awaited revelation:

to witness the great variety of shade
and shimmer, this endless radiance.

Those birds I thought I saw, but didn't—
now the towhee's rufous feathers gleam,

the solitaire's white-ringed eye
sharp as the black and white tweed

of a coat at the far end of the room,
clear as whites of that young man's eyes.

Blurred outlines sharpened, assumed
reality replaced by the truly real, every

wound on this aspen's pearled trunk
become a calligraphic scroll. I had not

known how completely a cloudy lens
dulled colors, stole defining details.

I'll return, see the smudged rosettes
on a leopard's coat, its blood-dried fur,

pietra dura on the royal tombs in Agra,

every sliver of stone on a single flower,

the glitter of waves foaming on rocks
below the wild green Cliffs of Moher.

Frozen Apples

Dawn. Open your eyes. Don't rise. Nothing waits
for you, no daily routine. As if you had
always lived alone. Stillness, so you can
hear the awakenings: first light, rose-streaked sky.
Through bare-limbed apricots you see the fields,
gone now to copper, mustard, muted green. How apples
hang on brown-leafed limbs, one tree bowed with the weight
of unpicked yellow apples. How they die in stages,
pale gold to cinnamon to shriveled rust. A few apples
rest half-buried in winter grasses. Don't think of waste,
of those who yearn for fruit, for crisp ripe apples. Don't
think of them. See only red, and one tree of yellow apples
turned the color of cider. So many rotted. If you could
gather them—but the time has past, they've frozen,
thawed, frozen again. Be grateful for one, half-firm,
half-spoiled, its flesh parting to the knife, its sweet juice,
the skin translucent on the ruined part. Be grateful
for the way light caught bronzed apples on the branches.
They looked beautiful—yes, for a moment, and ice
in the acéquia was a sheet of silvered
marble, patterns cracked like lace across the top.

A Vase of Flowers

11/9/16

You'd judge them humble,
flowers chosen
from a metal bucket by the market door,
arranged in a handmade vase
with white horses on the front and back,
set on the old half-moon commode, intricate
inlaid wood, faded cupids a century old.
Here the sensual Asiatic lily—
exposed throat, wide-flung petals,
overpowering scent, here pink and purple
clusters of Matsumoto mums.
When the showy lilies finish, pistils
spewing turmeric-colored pollen,
dust that stains your clothes and fingers,
these charming filler flowers
will offer themselves, the always-there ones.
Unobtrusive, they cede honored place
to the ostentatious scene stealers,
those privileged lilies. I know
from past bouquets
the stems won't wither until all the mums
have bloomed—purples, a few pinks—
small composites implying comfort,
a few blossoms I'll transfer to a tiny vase.
What if I leaned toward them,
our shared commiseration, a gift
expressing what my reticence keeps buried,
compassion deeper than rifts the dark days expose,
a gesture to ease shock and sorrow?
Don't they eventually open as fully
as they can, release spent petals to the glass?
Won't they rise up before they die?

Sustained

When you realize wildflowers reappear
after drought, when you find them risen
after a blessed spring of rain and snow,

rare wood lilies blooming among ferns
and deadfall, when you discover
one orange petal opened by rotted logs,

a single spark, not a wildfire that burns
the forest down, when you trust the earth
will green again, charred hillsides

regenerate, the net of aspens push up
new shoots, then you may choose to leave
your comfort, deny your resignation,

re-enter the vibrant world, then you will
embrace equally a child's soft, unblemished
skin and the creasing of your own face,

the blue-grey lichen crusted on a rock
and the gold pod of a withered iris,
both the bleached skull of a dead deer

and the living deer at the meadow's edge,
then you will rejoice as the Earth rotates,
celebrate how sun sears this land,

burns your skin, awakens fertile soil,
coaxes from it drowsing seeds to feed you,
gives you all the sustenance you need.

Enigma of Stone and Line

What are these stones stacked
by trails, on ridges, beside a stream, if not shrines
to manage loss and suffering,

cairns to guide an uncertain path? I add
a stone at times, milk-white to honor a little girl,
to wish her joyful steps along the way,

a green stone to ease my worries,
obsidian's dark luster for reasons not clear—
its antiquity, a coal waiting to ignite.

Today I saw graffiti on a concrete block
beside a stream. Isn't that all right, embellishment
on manmade failure, a broken base

that supported a structure no longer there,
the painted figure puzzling, not comfort, not threat?
A giant eye enclosed in densely sprayed

curves and spikes seemed to gaze beyond
the now-depleted stream, implying a seer's despair,
weariness at human-caused disaster.

When I climbed in front it looked through me
as if staring at mystery I couldn't see, a god's eye
stolen from a monument, perhaps salvaged

from a blown-up temple—a black enigma
depicted on the damaged block, light filtered across it
through a canopy of dying leaves.

Bedrock

at the International Folk Art Market

To walk past forest pines
beside the late-flowing stream
is to behold green abundance

despite drought-stunned lands
far east of here, and farther south,
another hemisphere, distant people—

the woman from South Sudan
in her multi-colored beaded dress,
her dignity layered beneath

turmoil, a never-yielding base,
telling us of recurring slaughter
in her chronically convulsed world,

of the inconsistency of food,
meaning hunger I can't imagine,
hunger in nations with no fields

to resurrect, no crops to harvest
for the rejoicing times, no
salvation in the cities, only praise

for these artists to carry home,
for the carved figures, woven cloths,
the joyous band from Mali singing

their dreams into the crowd, at this
market where we have eaten our fill,
where the woman, with her perfect

bones of Aphrodite, burns in anger
at the inequality of distribution,
here where the day finally cools

and the night sky rises, stars
attached to the vaulting dome, here
where we know rain will come.

Before Dawn

Four a.m. I've lost the moon to planet's tilt.
No reflected light through leafless branches.

No clouds. Stars' sheer crystals pasted
to the sky. The last car passed by long ago.

Why am I awake? Again. Everyone else
must be asleep. One light flickers in a window

down the street. Another soul walking
through the night. This is my peace-time,

my time for solitary wander. My nighttime
daydreams. A hush no one's voice disturbs.

Shadows fall outside the streetlamp's glow,
one leaf, bigger than my hand, spins across

the yard. My feet linger on bare wood,
my fingers touch a glass, an opened book.

Clouds begin to build, erasing stars. I found
one strip of moonlight, a glimmering line

across the floor slipped between two
half-closed slats. What am I excluding?

The Blank Page I Write On

At the entrance to the Burn
three trails diverge—
I chose the middle one,
descended in this buoyant season,
all dance and promise,
incantations of woodpeckers,
crows' cackle.

Now I look back, see what
is separate, distant—
black limbs of three dead cottonwoods
uphill from this confluence
of two streams choked with flood debris,
a filigree of aspen leaves
incised on flawless sky,
swirled like gold damascene
on the box I bought in Toledo, lost
as I lose so much I love,
even the language I worked
so hard to learn, until I dreamed
nocturnes in Spanish,
El Greco's reds and yellows,
the vibrant colors of Mexican murals.
Tongue and jaw shifted, framed
new words, rolled "r's," pronounced
the voiceless fricative of v and b.

Memory splinters,
leaves me here in the brilliant
mountain light I share
with clandestine creatures
that descend from nearby hills
at night, raccoons, the formal skunks,
these ravens banking overhead,
lecturing me in croaks
I'll never understand.

Mesa of Wind and Unceasing Light

The collared lizard startled, froze,
blended into pebbles and sand, scaled body
sallow as dirt, dry as the crusted soil,

still as grass while the cell phones caught him,
his seed-black eye, skin's speckled weave.
Circling overhead—above blight-killed

piñons, junipers spiraled like sculptures,
lightning-charred snags—three vultures drifted,
their wing tips gauzy as lace, shadows

over shadows. Our presence disturbed the life
of the mesa, miles plumed with bunch grass,
with cactus and dust, trails crisscrossing,

erasing. We wandered through a million
prickly pear spines, wine-red flares
of claret cups like the glimpse of an afterlife,

everything singing, and I moved away
from the others, a quiet at the edge, to gaze out
by a shrine of balanced rocks. Buried ashes

no longer see, but once had been here,
heart and bone, looking out from these cliffs,
this distance falling away into nothing.

Wild Irises

At Jack's Creek—
late spring deluge of irises, meadows
turned to purple lakes, a flood
to wade through.

Bending close we see
in every just-opened flower
what looks like brushwork—
fine lines pulled through lavender fall,
butter-yellow patch,
hues ranging from white's cool
composure to richest purple—saint's robe,
a Medici's cloak, the unsolved mystery
of Rome's imperial purple dye.

Mountain's silk threaded
through a deadfall meadow, so many
irises at their peak we give up counting,
testament to nurture, awe,
good fortune. Our visit timed
to catch the brief perfection—
exact hour, position of the sun,
amount of rain that fell the night before.

To wander through massed iris
is to sense the brevity.
If we glance back, we might
find the petals shriveled, pods
hardened on brittle stalks,
a few seeds rattling inside.

Zone and Errand

I have an errand imminent to an adjoining zone
Emily Dickinson

I seek distant venues, new regions
to search for other than who I seem to be.
The process can't be too long—what does long mean?

How long before the volcano blows again,
black particles spewed like residue from a funeral urn,
sharp bone fragments, dusty ash.

My father's ashes drifted over anonymous red rock—
I knew of no place he truly loved.

How long before I wake to earlier dawn—

how long before the planet tips closer to the sun—

how long before the air never cools again—

how long before my errand becomes clear?

Today I count on stillness waiting at the reservoir,
willows' early-winter pink, black sheen
of fallen leaves sewn across the pond, nothing moving,
no red-winged blackbird, no Cooper's hawk, no snake.

Scaffold, Light

Ghost Ranch, NM

What sustains me?
I must see raw earth to know—
the layered cliffs of Abiquiu,
lavender, burnt umber—
naked scaffolding exposed, fragilities,
emptiness wind blows through.

Red dirt rises from my footsteps,
white crust crumbles on a fallen slab,
a sky-blue vein snakes across this rock.

In front of an approaching storm
the sheared top of Pedernal looms black on black.
To the east florescent cumuli.
Late fall cottonwoods gold,
gold beside a debris-clogged creek.

Capstone, pinnacle, slot canyon
born of fault and shudder—
harsh erosions,
pitted rocks, stacks,
a juniper high on the cliff face,
roots nourished in a slender groove.

These roads of light
knit the earth together—
for this moment
I walk a luminous continuum
between the ordinary, the fantastic.

The Last Orchard

Parallel rows
to the straight
boundaries

planted
as if balance
assured renewal

shallow ditches
between the symmetry
of dormant trees

that obey the natural
progression of seasons
bud to flower to fruit

mornings I would
pause along a sun-lit row
retrieve a fallen peach

the anticipation
of pleasure concealing
for an instant

the shadows on the house
at the south corner
its burden of empty rooms

disguised by
the sweet fragrance
of ripened fruit

so delicious
when the flesh
was in my mouth.

Build a New House Within

Use sticks from your bones, color the walls
with red from your beating heart—shades of brick,
crimson, carmine, pull the lining from pale flesh
that never sees the light,

find, too, material from the dry land you live in:
hot pink prickly pear,
silver-grey berries on winter juniper,
the lightning streak of goldfinch wings.

Honor the high desert—here Earth's mass
folded outward, molten core heaved up
and cooled—minerals
flecked through rusty black—

make your house of this world, discard
the ruined one, stained by disappointment,
anger shredding the beams, pipes
rusted by depression—no matter how
you overlay it, the crumbling scaffold
will betray you—cracked plaster, a leaking roof—

start now before the ribs break,
the heart stops. After years
wasted patching the outer edifice,
there's time left to search below the crust,

the way a flashlight
shining in the blow hole
of a volcanic cone can reveal
deep corridors
you never dared explore.

ii.

Forgotten Language

After Constantine Cavafy

Didn't you say you would leave this city one day,
go back to another one you had loved, rescue
a forgotten language, let your heart beat
as it did before? Isn't that running away again?
Water strider, surface skimmer, seeking only
what pleases, why do you expect sky
of a different latitude to save you, your failures
to be shed like seed heads blown in the wind?

If you return, words will be strange
on your tongue, your accent wrong, the city
changed where *guardia civil* once stood
on every corner, a young artist
shouted *traidor* into the empty streets.

Isn't it time to give up regrets, daydreams
that arrive in the night? This is the city
you've lived in, mountains lining the eastern sky,
the thin luminous air, here you raised your sons,
saw the forests burn, reseed, turn green again.
Forget that city glazed by time. You threw away
only fantasy, aged walls of Moorish tiles,
Goya's demonic visions in the dark rooms
of the Prado, a king's ruined garden.
The *guardia civil*? No one in the city was free.

What Lies Behind

Kalaw, Myanmar

My eyes register only surface,
green health and grace,
all things fresh and gilded,
cauliflower, cabbage, flowering radish,
men and women hoeing,
no tractors,
no power lines,
no buzzing motor.

Bullock carts parked by the road.

Stillness, not even a bird.

To walk then to the Khmer village
on the long road up,
past fields, past forest shrines,
past houses raised on stilts,
to hear afterward, over tea,
what lies behind one man's weariness—

allusions to arrest, to fear,
to places I never look—

where the clouds went,
what lies behind burning rice straw,
behind white smoke rising in the fields,
behind the pastoral,
where I glance,
then see surface again—
whitewashed stupas beside the road,
gold-sprayed coconuts offered at a shrine.

Next Flight to Mandalay

In December fly west, go halfway around
the spinning globe, pack only what you can carry.

Arrive in Myanmar when the heat is bearable,
green fields checkered with cabbage, mustard,

flowering radish, the monsoon rains ended
so the dry plain of Bagan spreads before you,

three thousand pagodas visible through haze,
ancient bricks turned to fire in the setting sun.

May you find again what you came for—
to trade the empty spaces in your mind for this:

eight thousand golden statues of the Buddha
in the tunnels of a cave, lines of red-robed monks

with begging bowls, the sound of chanting at four a.m.
In Mandalay gaunt men pound gold to a molten state,

tissue-fine squares for gilding sacred shrines,
time measured by a lotus sinking in a pail of water.

Praise the ground you briefly walk upon,
the feel of temple floors beneath bare feet—

ceremonies witnessed in far off places where you,
a stranger, are welcome in the holiest of sites.

Dislocation

Myanmar

One moment I stood upright,
perpendicular as a tree, a pillar,
the next, I lay sprawled

on the water-slicked floor, such
force to wrench swiveling humerus
from its shallow cup of fiber

and nerves, a shift so radical,
so extreme—my reliable shoulder
unhinged, thousands of miles

from the tip of the southern Rockies
to the temple-strewn plain of Bagan,
where I still believed I could rise

and walk, every living bone
knit to its proper place, not lie undone
in a hospital of shadows and dust,

pain thrumming its unbearable din
until the gentle doctor arrived
wrapped in a cotton skirt

and took my hand, pulling
the skewed arm straight, pointing it
toward the star-laced dark

as if he offered me flight, the bone
eased back in its cradle. I had
drifted away to a place

of reverie and bliss, barely aware
of my son's voice chanting, the sound
of *om* calling me back, saving

the journey, so our travels continued,
the steps of a thousand pagodas
waiting for us to ascend.

Red Warbler

The mountain garlanded
with trees, its cryptic face,
the folds and furrows, unchanging—
it rises up and up—
and there, paused by the stone-stepped path,
jewel fastened to a branch,
a bird red as cranberry in a bog,
as wild raspberry,
bright as blood oozed from a cut,
each cheek a peck of snow—
flutter, flit, a scarlet streak,
red as my wishes, my dreams last night.
Perched above the broken stones,
the treacherous path,
a flash through the woven, tangled trees,
little beacon, Christmas light,
a candle flame. Trees so thick-grown
the mountain's lost,
though I rise on the shadowed trail
threaded through branch and leaf, up and up.
How I would love to borrow
those fiery wings,
feel them float up the massive cliffs,
carry me to the pyramid on top—
if only I could shift to flight,
not continue on these human feet,
this slow, deliberate, step by step.

Nonfiction

Though I wish that he, Raghu,
had been symbolic, like the tailors
in Rohinton Mistry's novel,
one of the millions of India's poor
who rise from ash,
the beautiful transcending,
that his brief life did not conform
to the arc of tragedy,
that his grace still dignified
the dust and heat of Ahmedabad,
that he still rode his bicycle
adapted for legs withered by disease,
still delivered the gift of meals
to widowed women who daily waited for him,
his smile their lives' small sun,

and I wish that his luck's
inconstant light had not faded,

that his personal gods had spared him
in the din of horns and screaming brakes,
that his belief in temples, priests,
ringing bells, in *Upar Wala*, the One Above,

still sustained him, that the hand-sewn banner
he gave my son had not lost
a portion of its joy, that the fabrics
of silk and cotton, bits of mirror,
bells and beads, had not darkened
in my mind, each piece
shadowed by the knowledge
of the oncoming—swerve,
collide, the shear of metal on metal,
the crush of metal on bone.

They Sell Souls in the Marketplace

In this village you can
buy a soul, they sell them
in birdcages, here where they say
magic still exists, lingers near
the twelfth century pyramid
high on the mountain's
sculpted slopes, filters
through the still-clear air.

Some cages hold birds—
there, a goldfinch,
his feathers like tamped flames,
trills pouring through his prison bars.
Other cages trap a soul inside—
poor fluttering absences,
struggles, sorrows.
The vendor assures me
if I buy one, the freed soul
will bless my home.

Embroidered cloths cover
the cages, hide what cries inside.
A soul's size must vary—
a child's gauzy as a dragonfly,
an adult's larger, broad
as an oriole's spread wings;
surely they press against the bars,
beg you to release them.
Is there only belief to fill the cage,
only my desire to perform
one kindness without regret,
my hope to be blessed
by what may rise?

Would you yourself buy a soul?

Casa de Linares

Madrid, 1963

December, every day darker, colder.
Intermittent snow, my gloved hands freezing
when I walked to the antique store
where I worked, hired for my English,
how perfectly you speak, the tourists said.
On slow days, the other workers took turns
conversing, the infinite patience
of their corrections, a kind coaxing out
of words until language began to bloom.
How I loved pronouncing the Castilian lisp,
tongue between the teeth: /θ/ *cinco.*
On the sidewalks, the long, lingering residue
of civil war, despondent men dressed in grey,
a limb missing, a mutilated face—
the chestnut seller on the corner,
the man who swept the streets, the man
begging in the nearly-deserted park.
I remember early mornings, the store
not yet opened, a few gypsies always waiting
by the door. Dark men, dark clothes.
Furtive. I watched their long coats open,
reveal the stolen pieces they brought to sell.
A tarnished silver bowl, a carved saint
with bleeding hands, a gold necklace.
No questions, more antiques to stock the shelves.
Provenance unknown. Still, I learned
to speak more fluently, learned
to nod politely to the *guardia civil*, learned
to eat roast chestnuts sold in paper cones,
to look past the bullet holes in walls,
to place my few pesetas in a poor man's
outstretched hand, to discuss Goya's demons
with the man who washed the Prado's floors.

Return Trip

The weary Ángel
unable to raise her corroded wings,
the city sinking back into its ancient lakebed,
the water going, so many thirsty people
gasping to wet their lips.

I follow perimeters
of where I used to walk, avoid old footprints,
the university, the streets I lived on,
avoid the monuments—all changed,
pass lines of armed men near the Zócalo,
machine guns, riot gear, body shields,
a platoon of police as if they were
black-clothed trees, a bleak forest—unchanged,
armed men and the lines of protestors—
placards and shouts, *Peña Nieto traidor*—
or were they silent, did I dream
my past, time turned back, the city
always in turmoil, sinking, the sky soiled,
a tangle of unmanageable highways
rising and falling through murk.
I'll never find the volcanos, never walk
on broad boulevards, through green parks—

though somewhere the air is clear, somewhere
transparent, somewhere I'll find flowers
singing in the daytime dusk—
hibiscus, bougainvillea, poinsettia—
where once I found beautiful words,
the writers sending their words
into the hazed light, powerful, fired with force,
to strike a target, peel back a façade.
Killing no one.
And the words are still written,
the city sinking, ornate structures undulating,

fighting to stand, and water,
the precious essential water, almost gone.

A Ceramic Bowl, A Tiny Urn

Ocuituco, 16th Century

They never left Mictlán, the Place
of Death; sun never warmed their face.
Tiny bones of Aztec twins,
remains of ceremony to honor never-birth,
two infants nestled in a ceramic bowl,
fallen from the womb,
premature, unfulfilled, unbloomed—
expelled before the organs worked, before
the hearts pumped on their own.

San Diego, 2011

Too-early birth, the lost twin, a boy,
his frail bones unpreserved,
a tiny urn to hold the fist of ashes—
his parents chose a serene site
high above the sea,
to acquiesce, accept
their son would have a life not-life.
Hands outspread, they shared his ashes
with the sky, mourned their flight,
a faint trail drifting above roses,
camellias, bird of paradise.

Tepoztlán, 2017

In the museum of the Ex-Convento
lie fetal bones five centuries old—
they seemed small animals—a rabbit,
perhaps a squirrel—what skin
once covered such delicate ribs,
papery cerebral plates, spines
like spider webs? Small gaps show
where a missing bone would go.
They rest in separate cases. Displayed

beside them—the ceramic bowl.

San Diego, 2017

The twin who lives, a joyful girl
now five, airborne, gossamer, child
with honey-shining hair.
Pink glasses give her perfect sight,
she sees her world, though edges blur.

Turn your head, little one, you'll find
all the seagulls you love to chase,
all the ponies waiting for you to ride,
all the bright lemons on your tree—
so many dazzling yellow suns.

iii.

Immersed

Why have you climbed here again   alone
above the blue lake   this purity
of high mountain water
a scramble to reach the tarn   a hollowed bowl
spring fed   snow melt   almost a mouth calling

here a raven's view   as if   flight
were possible   wingless soaring   over pines
deadfall   wildflowers   in meadows   trailside   along streams
sky pilot   fringed gentian   heart-leaf arnica's   gold suns

from the ridge   turn-back is farther than miles left   to complete the loop
descend to the lake   clear   cold   immerse your hand
to cleanse in wilderness

retrace familiar steps   one foot after the other   again and again
while there is still time   not like the passing of years

mist tatters into sky   clouds unstitch
slopes erode   blue fingers reach toward   shaded drainage

as the day clears   green canopy   breaks up the light
come down   the deep mouth urges   before the cloud rebuilds

old stories become possible   on this long journey   more mistakes
claws   paw prints   a footstep in the mud   if you take the wrong trail

now the sun's angle shifts   what can change you   radiance
the blue lake calling   come down

Outcrop with Vision, No Sound

His fingers shaped language

signing triumph   forming joy
as if words couldn't touch all he saw

silence enshrined
in the jumbled rocks   the crags
the brittle green of juniper and piñon

we knew nothing   not his name   his life
one brief exchange

something deep released there
altering us   who saw his rapture

ridges snow-dusted
mother-of-pearl

red granite scattered in the dust
marbled like raw meat

trail no longer windswept   a brief settling
and though the insight will vanish
there were no sufferings   no conflicts

young man descending the rock outcrop
summit of a minor peak

hard to stop the mind   its invented stories

then there's the swift
surprising notice   the ability to simply see

Flute in Yellow Woods

Our footfalls cushioned
in residue and rot,
we follow a ragged stream,
the aspens wind-swayed,
falling leaves pinned like sequins
to the pine boughs.

Lovely the trees' black-etched
flaws, the scars left
by broken limbs.

The season's cusp, a turn
before the end, as if I myself
might choose the final passage,
a spiraling flight
through perfect clarity.

At the granite upthrust
we find handholds,
wedge our toes
into shallow niches,

this, the ascent above rushing water
toward a higher threshold.

Across the stream one man
searches among bronzed plants
for something unnamed,
strapped on his back a flute
whose notes we'll never hear.

Erratic gusts strip off
a storm of tarnished leaves,
the shift from stillness
foretelling winter's
cold, unpeopled woods.

Unlike Byzantium

Near the coppery rocks I think of Byzantium,
of kings, of artifacts, of hammered gold—
an ark containing a golden bird, a key
to animate him. The ancient world
of rulers, craftsmen, ore—

but I'm here by cliffs
rising from a canyon where water
rarely runs, sand rippled at the edges,
piled debris—flash flood legacy—
and these massive rocks
not forged by artisans, not a pounded arc,
a plated box—they rose from heaves,
folds, volcanic explosions—
eons to make these rifts, ledges,
diagonals, breaks—

and the sun-struck faces shine—
seared blacks, rusted bronze, ochre—
in places slabs broke and fell,
slits opened. You can proceed to a deeper place,
ascend the rocks, I'm told,
if you dare the darkness.
A way up is there for you, waiting.
No elegant clothes required,
no gold to pay for viewing gold.
How much courage does ascension ask?
See, there are scales by the opening
in the fence. Weigh yourself
before you enter, make sure
your heart contains sufficient grams.

In the Aftermath of Flood

You know the roar tumultuous water made,
the din of breakage,

crushed building blocks of cliffs, fallen layers
of saffron, ochre, rose,

the immensity of one cottonwood torn up
by roots, wedged between

canyon walls, the sculptured twist, its limbs
adorned with river stones,

car-sized boulders jammed in slots like ramparts
built against a siege—

residue of cataclysm engraved in sandstone walls,
a template of destruction,

wreckage that illustrates how the eternal-seeming
can easily be torn apart.

Here witness the silent spectacle of what remains—
moss-grown seepage glistening

like sheets of glass, resurrected plants, new bends
in the river bed,

a slab of cracked red rocks clinging to the cliff,
a solitaire calling

from an untouched pine. Now praise the canyon,
your innocence, your awe.

Cyclical

The aspens' brass-bright leaves
anticipate stripped limbs,
frozen earth, the diminishing of light—

make of the sequence what you wish—
seasonal death before spring resurrection,
the inevitable rhythm, or is it
the art of dying?

This red-leafed bush, worn out
by its summer fires, has only embers left.

I'm trying to guess
how it feels to take your leave
if you have no leaves to drop
spinning to the ground.

I myself have minerals
sluicing from my bones, pigment
slipped from once dark hair,
a linear progression woven
through recurring cycles—
yesterday flash floods in the arroyo
carved a deeper channel,
and last week
another massive slab
peeled from the cliff behind me—

daily shifts between catastrophe
and infinite regeneration
that connect what begins
to all that ends—
and then begins again.

Waiting for Strangers

I have fallen on the rocks
of eroded trails and found more
inspiration in the dirt
under my hands
than on the broken streets
of my city.

When I walk alone
there is no sound but wind,
a half-fallen tree creaking
against a broken branch.

I take the wrong turn,
stray off the path,
the marked trail—
have you ever
misplaced your car,
failed to notice a street sign,
wandered at dusk in a foreign city,
felt your face as visible
on a crowded street as the hawk
turning now in an empty sky?
Doesn't a stranger always
step forward, lead you away
from the narrow lane,
the blind alley?

In countless cities
and towns and villages
I venture past the known route,
the easy descent, hoping to find
destinations to speed my heartbeat—
places past the guard rail,
the guide's advice.
I want the light shifted,
the mind charged, I want
to know that when I turn back—
yes, I will be changed.

Messages

Listening to the body's hints—
is there something I should pay attention to?
Do I heed what the stressed trees tell, the dying bees,
the dead fox in the canyon?

The years fly on, people wither,
fade as if they were leaves—those dropping now,
chlorophyll blocked the way pigment
ceases coloring hair,
an exhaustion in the mechanism.

Years ago perception shifted—
the mantra: *things are not as they seem.*
When I scored ellipses on a sheet of card stock,
the creases yielded differently than my eyes
predicted, than my mind grasped,
the stiff paper curling into a graceful loop—
now I expect that the surface
often belies the truth.

Aung Sang Suu Kyi, winner
of the Nobel Peace Prize, allowed slaughter
of the Rohingya people.
Don't look at the world, blood spilled
from bodies, somewhere another species
dying, so many of us crowded here—

dawn arrives each morning,
and yesterday among rocks and gullies
the flock of bluebirds—
I would never tell them how brief their stay is—
plain, greyish birds
flitting branch to branch—
then light caught their wings
and everywhere brilliant indigo flashed.

The Angel Leaves

When the angel fasting inside you has grown so thin...
Larry Levis

It slips out the flushed tips of your fingers—first,
pressure, then a twinge, the way my body hurt
in adolescence, changing. Discomfort in the bones.

As if I felt childhood's exit, flow of my own blood,
the silent work of cells: slough and renewal, steady pump
of the heart at night. This departure similar, an ache,

an ethereal presence leaving—was I even aware of it?
A buoyancy I ignored, indifferent. It must pass
through the skin—spirit permeating a membrane, brief

illumination you may notice if the time is right.
Just before twilight perhaps, the dreamy, pensive end of day
when you are most receptive to gradations of hue.

A shadow stretching in front of me, wavering,
malnourished. Could I reach out to touch it,
make amends, offer purpose, my whole attention?

Sudden shifting intensity of light, a different quality—
gold layered onto black. The fingers swelling, then
a vacancy, my body emptied. Not quite hunger,

but as if something essential abandoned me, a truth
I had neglected. I'm left with afterimage, brightness
on the retina. The angel I'll miss for the rest of my life.

Threshold

Listen. Be receptive
to the waves of not-sound—
let them slip through
porous skin, slide across
a strand of hair—

not the rattle of a village day,
not an old truck bouncing down
a cobbled street,
not vendors' chants,
the soft slap of their huaraches
by a café door. Not those.
Lean your ear toward
the unheard sounds—beyond
tone, timbre, whisper,
under the voice, the note, the rustle—

then you may hear the shimmering
of the air, the mountain
stretching out
its creased and folded face,
the sound of light spilling down
the rocks, shadows
shifting with the sun,
an oriole rising from the stream.

Not the swish, the almost-creak
stiff feathers make,
but the felt trace left by his breast's
stoked fire, the visual
remade through windless air—
two clarities joined—
silence singing past the silence
until his raucous call
splits stillness into shards.

iv.

The Black-billed Magpies

Talpa, NM

In the leaf-choked acéquia,
a magpie paused.
His wings gleamed
iridescent green,
then blue.

*

Once in Ireland
I had longed for magpies.
I heard them
in the lime trees—
they flew everywhere
through rain.

*

It was a time
the too-early baby
lay far away, her
breathing measured
by a wavering green
erratic line.

*

The nursery rhyme says
one for sorrow,
two for joy,
three for a girl—

a fourth one came;
he couldn't stay.

*

Which pleasure
do I prefer—
desire or fulfillment?
Not the first magpie
in the treetop,
but the windblown
tiding, whirling
overhead.

*

Why can't I live
with sorrow?

*

My life
does not depend
on the flight
of magpies
in a winter orchard,
their zigzagged glide
above these frozen
apple trees.

*

Today's weather—
overcast and cold.
More snow predicted.
Two ravens
swoop back and forth
across the grey.
All the magpies
have flown away.

*

It's time for me to leave.

Cranes

At sunset, despite clouds covering the sun,
the sky turned pink deepening to violet,
and when the sandhill cranes in the fields,
though not the thousands we hoped to see,
rose in their orderly formations
to choose the water they would sleep on,
they turned to pearl then gold as they passed
overhead. Ducks dabbled in the waterways—
not merely ducks as I had called them—
they were busy shovelers and pintails, coots
and buffleheads, and a flush of startled mallards
flew over winter fields of cinnamon and rust.

At dawn the marsh was a metal plate
stippled with coppery rushes,
just visible as the sliver of sky widened,
a blue crevice gradually giving us light,
and the sun appeared at last, high already
above the hills. Massed by the shore,
snow geese gleamed white as china.
As we left, three cranes posing by the road
turned to show us the red skin on their heads,
like rubies or blood, red as the last apples
flaming on a bronze-leafed tree.

Walking the Reservoir

The tawny colors seem neither death nor sleep,
though their depleted radiance—
dun, rust, copper—leans into this slanted light.

Metallic reeds embrace the pond,
one blue chickweed blooming, sky-specked,
a tangle of unfinished beaver work,
still-green elm leaves laced by insect bites.

Everything dust and dry,
cottonwood and willow yearning
for the next rain,
only a shallow trickle of released water
in the now-restored channel.

Along the bank dried grasses
flicker like slender torches—
once a friend taught me all the names.
When I remember some—
side oats, little blue stem, threeawn—
I have him back again, morning walks
with dogs, Bill patiently repeating grasses.

From the north rim the marsh looks milky green,
a bronze patina of fallen leaves seamed
like a plaque laid over melted glass.

Today I didn't see a single bird.

Skater

Night, a full moon.
Or perhaps it's waning.
The skating rink
at the mountain's crest,
flat top of Squaw Peak carved
against the star-ticked dark.

She's steadied
by the skater's arms, a boy
she'll never see again.
His strength borrowed until
her blades balance on the ice,
a solid base from which
she'll fly, confident
on the irregular surface
of everything that lies ahead.

New snow, each faceted flake
unique as the irises of an eye.
The purifying, containing
cold. Shadowed trees
beyond the illuminated rink,
then the raven-dark.

His arm around her waist,
moonlight reflecting off the ice.

A boyhood spent skating
on frozen streams and ponds,
like figures in Bruegel's painting.
Not the lean hunters
with their starved dogs,
but a single figure spinning
on the ice, the landscape
frigid, sunless.
One skater near the far edge,
mist sprayed up behind his blades.

Sampler

Once my hair shone, not a raven's wing—
highlights caught the sun,
as light always
shines through darkness,
soft glow of candle flame,
moon's white stroking the lawn.

Can you absorb the purity of dawn,
be like waterbirds waking in the marsh,
deer in a valley of foxtails?

Textured collages in a light-filled studio:
bubble wrap and gauze, wire and paint,
staple, twist, stitch, fold.

I came from arid land, dry
as the blood in my veins, thistle and dandelion,
seed heads floating like cotton.

Who climbed a temple with me in Yangon,
who sat in the bar with me in Getaria,
who ran with me to catch the Seville train?

My once-blank page, crisscrossed,
rewritten, is almost filled—
here I'll draw my iconic bird,
wings like lace, gold thread worked
through feathers.

Now I can see if sky transforms him,
if he turns to fire when he flies.

Copper Leaf, Extinguished Fire

If I find nothing
in the room I wake,
monotony of the doves'
two note complaint, hush of heat-rise
out the window,
if I find
in the too-shaded garden only
stunted dahlias, the empty leaves of iris,
if I find
the backyard strip of sand
covered by thorned branches,
plum leaves, dust,
if I hear then
the finches' lilt,
their buoyant chatter,
if I see
a hummingbird sipping nectar
from red sage's thick-clustered cups,
I will recall
the copper leaf detaching
from a banyan tree high overhead—
the flutter of its slow descent.
I will trust there are gaps
for me to float through
the way the leaf drifted
into shafts of light, spinning
in a dying grace,
and if I pause to watch
the fading minutes of the day—
rose-streaked sky,
the sun's extinguished fire—
I can wait,
alone, for darkness.

Stepping Over the Brink

I forgot summer's green
veiled a different palette until I saw
this shift to yolk gold, mustard, pollen.

I'll go out now, late afternoon.
So much light intensified—
I won't look away.

My own skeleton, like my
reserve, masks the depths, dulls
internal luster. What have I saved it for?
I'll no longer stop
at the pumping heart, the lungs.

Before winter's hushed days
deter me, I'll remove a layer, reveal
the shimmering undercoat,
risk its glare, naked as the leaves
of these cottonwoods and aspens,
the single red vine wrapping chamisa
in fire—this euphoria,
ongoing celebration
until freeze seals off every stem,
sends brightness spinning,
leaf-lights hanging from the pines,
tarnished yellows pasted to the ground.

Last Autumn

I remember the autumn of 2016. Though it
might have been earlier. It seems like yesterday.

It was the autumn I gave up riding. Despite
how I loved the feel of a horse cantering,

the way my body yielded to every stride,
the times I could borrow a horse's grace.

It was the autumn the leaves stayed gold
for weeks—or were they ginger, rust,

the bronze that comes with dying? It was
the autumn I didn't miss green at all, rushes

bleached to dun around the pond, a silvery
scrim of fallen leaves settled on the water.

The maze of lines feathered across my palm
reflected the veins on every leaf I touched.

I remember uncertainty that autumn, how
tree rings hinted at messages I couldn't read.

Robins changed their song, vandals ruined
trail signs, all the cairns had toppled over,

and the one man I passed never smiled.
I realized then I had no idea where I was.

The Undefined

In August thunderstorms build
in the afternoon, a rumble like drums
far back in the hills. Once I heard a man

chanting beneath a rock outcrop. Once
I saw a man carrying his flute by a stream
where a taut wire prevented my crossing.

Once I saw sandhill cranes grazing
in fields of wheat, and migration called
to me, the lure of a foreign departure,

as yet undefined, which is also a freeing,
an urge to satisfy wonder, to coax beauty
out of the air, to live uncontained,

like snow light throughout the marsh, shining
as it waits for the mallards and pintails
to spread their wings, to lift from the reeds,

their ascent opening a shuttered casement
on the transcendence of flight, the broken
shells of emergence only remnants

to be scattered in rising winds. Though
it seemed as if sorrow had carried them off,
it could just as well have been joy.

Before the Flame Goes

Heritage of summer heat, ennui,
the time cicadas drone on and on, foxtails
stick to socks, prickly-pear spines glint,
a stab, blood drip, color of flowers spilling down a wall—
no—that was another country—
they mix, blend, confuse.

~

The mirror tarnishes.

~

An old man in his bed, my father, so yellowed
when we found him, he had departed long before,
just skin pulled over bones,
like the sacrificial statues in the Templo Mayor—
the skin of one body pulled over another,
strings of flesh knotted on the back,
a double death,

~

and yesterday 80 degrees reflecting off dry cliffs
felt hotter than 118 degrees in the Valley,
when it was too hot to cross a stifling room,
like the lassitude in Chichen Itzá, step by step
across the ball court, visiting
another ritual of death.

~

This life pleads for attention—
wood lilies' speckled throats,
pink mariposas, a rare red warbler weaving flame
through branches along broken cobbled steps,
a one thousand foot gain, straight up.

I bequeath myself, the poet wrote,
to grow from this stressed dry earth.
Ascend again, while you know descent
is possible to the beloved grass, greening now.

~

And the desert nights no longer cold in summer,
no winter coat needed for the opera—
arias and choruses pouring into open air—
the time lightning split the sky
at the exact moment Don Giovanni
was pulled down to Hell—
shouldn't all rapacious men end like that?
Flames' vengeance for all to see—
and the women free, bonds undone, radiant
in the star-blazed night, time enough
to sing gloriously before the stage goes dark.

Replay

See the myriad birds repeat
hours later when you close your eyes.

Images sort from layers
printed on the retina,
one frame projects, then another.

First, the snow geese gleam
on opaque water, porcelain bowls
that stir, settle, transform
into beak and wing, departure's
breathless whoosh, black shapes
against still-dark sky.
Focus then on foreground,
the coots' sable dabbling,
tail feathers lifted into frigid air.

Let the sandhill cranes
take flight again, undulant calligraphy
sketched across dawn sky.
A few stay to feed
in rivulets of marsh and grass,
feathers mud-preened, curved neck
crisscrossing curved neck.

Replay, then, sun's rising curve,
the half moon's slow erasure,
the way you turned, light
behind you, and rabbit brush
ignited, seed heads
sprayed with diamonds.
Do you see now that you too
were incandescent?

Deborah Casillas, originally from California, is a long-time Santa Fe Resident. She has a BA in English from UC Berkeley and an MA in Spanish language and Latin American literature from UNAM in Mexico City. In a writing workshop in Santa Fe years ago she discovered her passion for writing poetry. Since then she has attended workshops in Taos, Squaw Valley, Tomales Bay and Tepoztlán, Mexico. Her poems have appeared in various journals, including *Prairie Schooner, Silk Road Review, The Squaw Valley Review, Santa Fe Literary Review, North American Review, New Ohio Review, Whitefish Review, The Carolina Quarterly*, and an anthology from Tepoztlán, *Under the Volcano/Bajo el Volcán*.

www.ingramcontent.com/pod-product-compliance
Lightning Source LLC
Chambersburg PA
CBHW021201090426
42740CB00008B/1191